Pocl

Place

of Sheffield

Ron Clayton & Alistair Lofthouse

© Ron Clayton / Alistair Lofthouse 2009

Cartoons: Mychailo Kazybrid

Printed and published by:
ALD Design & Print
279 Sharrow Vale Road
Sheffield S11 8ZF

Telephone 0114 267 9402
E:mail a.lofthouse@btinternet.com

ISBN 978-1-901587-80-7

First published August 2009

A word or two about the need for Lofthouse and Clayton's Pocket Guide to the Place Names of Sheffield.

The biggest village in England is made up, like all big villages or cities, of umpteen former farms, villages, hamlets and places, largely merged into one.

Bearing in mind Sheffield has several place names like Portmahon, Portobello, Philadelphia, existent since the eighteenth century these are now completely unknown to the average Sheffielder. Also areas like Owlerton which has been merged into Hillsborough, itself a product of the late 18th/early 19th century, are no longer distinct. With this and the fact that the present day Sheffield lies in the ancient area known as Hallamshire [reference to David Hay's 'Historic Hallamshire'] whose boundaries are less than crystal clear to others, apart from the dedicated local historian or publisher of local history books, it is clear that a pocket guide to Sheffield place names for Sheffielders old and new is required. Something not just for the weekend but in the pocket/dashboard as you commute during the working week or in backpack/bike jacket during leisure time.

This Pocket Guide will help make sense of Sheffield, Past and Present and put meat on the bones of those areas identified only by the 'Welcome To' signs erected recently by a city once again on the move.

Many of our suggestions are subject to opinion, so if you disagree or you can supply more information regarding any place names please write to us at:

ALD Design & Print
279 Sharrow Vale Road
Sheffield S11 8ZF

Beauchief Abbey

Abbeydale

Takes its name from the fact that Beauchief Abbey is situated in the valley that is known as Abbeydale.

Arbourthorne

Means shelter formed by trees.

Attercliffe

A place at a cliff, maybe higher ground. East side of the River Don

1

Banner Cross

The base of an old stone cross still remained at Banner Cross in 1819. Addy in 1888 suggested that the name derives from bæna kross, meaning the cross of prayers.

Beauchief

A famous example of local dialect, being pronounced Beuchief. The name is from Norman times hence French 'Beuchef' meaning 'the beautiful head'. The area is dominated by Beauchief Abbey founded around 1176. The Abbey was a Premonstratensian order where there were Canons instead of monks. The Abbey was closed in 1537 by Henry VIII and today only the bell tower remains as a church plus extensive foundations.

Beighton

Known in the 13th century as Becton. Beck is the name for a stream in old English (still used) so the meaning is village by the stream.

Bents Green

Named after a type of course grass known as 'bent grass'. It must have grown locally.

Birley

From old words Byrley meaning cowshed and leah meaning forest clearing.

Carbrook Hall 1819, E. Blore

Brightside

The Bright family had their home at Carbrook Hall, now a pub. Colonel Bright fought on the side of Cromwell in the English Civil War.

Bradfield

Wide treeless area.

Bradway

Meaning 'broad way' or, in other words, wide road.

Brincliffe

Thought to come from two old words, 'brende' meaning clearing produced by burning and 'clif' meaning steep hill.

Broomhall

Taking its name from the hall that has existed in varoius forms for over 500 years. Restored in the 1960s by Sheffield designer David Mellor.

Broomhill

Takes name from a house built by William Newbould in 1792 near to where Newbould Lane is today. He called the house 'Broomhill' as it was the first house above Broomhall and it was on a hill.

Burngreave

A grove (or wood) by a stream.

Carsick

Marshy area with stream running through it.

Chapeltown

In the middle ages known as 'Chappell' meaning chapel there.

Commonside
Land by area of common land.

Crookes
Said to be from an old Norse word for a corner of land, "Krokr".

Crookesmoor
Large open space near Crookes. Was home to Sheffield race course many years ago.

Crosspool
Where the roads crossed the pools from times when Crosspool was just moorland.

Crystal Peaks

Most bizarre of all Sheffield place names, sounds like a cult American TV series. Part of Mosborough new town, planned in the 1960s but built in the 1970s/80s.

Darnall

Secluded nook of land.

Deepcar

An area of marshy, boggy land with a few trees. First mention of Deepcar is in 1771.

Dore

Dore

Mentioned in Anglo Saxon documents as far back as AD829, the name means narrow pass and is famous for the point at which King Ecgbert unified the United Kingdom when the Northumbrians surrendered to him in AD827.

Ecclesall Church 1850

Ecclesall

From old English 'Eccles halh' meaning 'church in the hollow'. Ecclesall church nowadays is not in a hollow but an earlier building was. Often miss-spelt 'Eccleshall' even by Sheffield City Council who, in the 1980s, had some road signs thus spelt!

Ecclesfield

Eccles is the old British word for Church, as in Ecclesall, therefore the village is the church in the field.

Firth Park

An area that surrounds Firth Park that was land donated by Mark Firth in 1875 for public use. Mark Firth was a Sheffield steel pioneer whose company Firth Brown was very important to Sheffield. Mark wished to create a good environment for his workers, not unlike the Bourneville project near Birmingham created by Cadbury's.

Gates to the Firvale Workhouse

Firvale

The valley below Fir Hill. The Northern General Hospital was originally the Fir Vale Workhouse.

Frecheville

Named after a Norman family who held the area for some 600 years.

Fulwood

Apparently means 'dirty wood' in old English!

Gleadless

Bird clearing.

Greenhill

In the 12th century know as Greenhilheg, just means a logical green hill! Part of Derbyshire until 1934.

Greenland

Named after nearby fields called 'Far Green Lane' and 'Near Green Lane'.

Grenoside

From old English 'Grafan' meaning to dig, and old Norse 'Haugr' meaning hill so in other words, 'Place of the Quarries'.

Greystones

May have been named after a local outcrop of rocks but possibly 'Grey Stones' were used as boundary markers in England during Saxon times.

Grimesthorpe

Named after remote a farm owned by the Grim family.

Hackenthorpe

Similar to above, Hacken's farmstead.

Handsworth

The land once belonged to someone called 'Hand' about 900 years ago.

Heeley

Was known as Heghlegh meaning high clearing.

Hemsworth

Land belonging to 'Hemele' in a similar way to Handsworth.

Herdings

High clearing in woods.

High Green

Area of high land.

Highfield

A common name for a field.

Hillsborough

Originally known as 'The Hills', there is an area in Northern Island called Hillsborough, strangely enough there is an Orange Lodge in Hillsborough that marches from Hillsborough Hall to Wadsley War Memorial.

Hollinshead

Appears to be connected with Holly which had been grown there for winter food for animals.

Hunter's Bar

From John Hunter who had a farm in the area around 400 years ago. The 'Bar' must be from when there was a toll bar where the junction between Ecclesall Road and Brocco Bank is today. A copy of the toll bar is preserved on the roundabout.

Hutcliffe Wood

Named after local wood whose old name was 'Huda's Cliff.

Intake

Area of land taken in for agriculture.

Jordanthorpe

Jordan's farm.

Kelham Island 2009

Kelham Island

Named after a Mr Kellam Homer who, in 1674, owned a workshop and water wheel located on what is today Kelham Island. Records show he was the town armourer in 1637. His water wheel became known as Kellam Wheel and by the early 1800s with a change of spelling the island was given the same name.

Lodge Moor

Taking its name from a hunting lodge belonging to the Earl of Shrewsbury.

Longley

'Longlegh' meaning long clearing.

Lowedges

Named after a farm located in the area called Lowedges Farm.

Lowfield

As the name suggests, the name of a field in the area.

Loxley

From old English meaning forest glade owned by Locc. Local legend has it that Robin Hood came from this area!

Malin Bridge

After the former land owner of the area 'Malin Stacie'.

Manor

Comes from the Earl of Shrewsbury's Manor Lodge built in the area. The Earl owned Sheffield Castle but wanted a more comfortable place to live. Mary Queen of Scotts spent

Manor Lodge (part of) 1898 by A. Wilson

about a third of her 14 years of captivity in Sheffield at The Manor. Only ruins remain now.

Manor Top

High ground above the Sheffield Manor.

Meadowhead
Simply top of the meadow.

Meersbrook
Takes its name from the stream 'Meers Brook'. For a long time the stream was the dividing point between Yorkshire and Derbyshire. Mere is another name for boundary.

Middlewood
May be from a wood in the middle of Wadsley.

Millhouses
Simply means houses by the mill, the mill was located in what is now Millhouses Park.

Mosborough
From Moresbury meaning fort on the hill.

Neepsend
In old Norse 'nypr' meaning peak and 'end' being added as Neepsend lies at the end of a high ridge. By the 17th century the area was known as Nypysend.

Nether Edge

Taken from a name of a farm whose buildings later became The Brincliff Oaks pub. There were two farms locally; Nether Edge Farm and Upper Edge Farm, nether meaning lower.

Nether Green

Similar to Nether Edge, meaning lower green.

Netherthorpe

Norse settlement.

Norton

Once the northern most parish of the Scarsdale Hundred of Derbyshire, 'North-ton' became part of Sheffield in 1900.

Norwood

Simply north wood as opposed to say south wood or east wood.

Oughtibridge

In the early years of the 12th century a ford existed across the Don which was controlled by a man named Oughtred. When, in around 1150 a bridge was built, it was known as 'Oughtred's Bridge' or perhaps by his nickname, Oughty's Bridge.

Owlerton

J. Edward Vickers suggested Alor-tun a farmstead by the elders, nothing to do with Owl in the tree that was once the badge of Sheffield Wednesday!

Parkhead

The highest part of the old manorial park owned by Sir Robert de Ecclesall.

Parkhill

The last of Sheffield's seven hills to be built upon, was part of Sheffield's great deer park owned by Lord of the Manor, The Earl of Shrewsbury.

Parsons Cross

Possibly from a roadside preaching cross used until the reformation. Stocksbridge may have been the site of a similar cross.

Philadelphia

Named after the American state, which was part of British empire at the time.

Pitsmoor

An area of pits or holes where ore was dug from the ground. An early indication of one of the reasons why Sheffield became the 'City of Steel'.

Portmahon

The name commemorates a battle in the Napoleonic Wars that happened off Port Mahon on Minorca.

Portobello

Scene of British Victory against the Spanish in 18th Century.

Ranmoor

Ranmoor

From Rand Moor. Rand may have meant border so meaning moor by boundary.

Ringinglow

Could be named after an ancient monument. There are many lows in Derbyshire that are from ancient times. Ringing could suggest that this structure was circular.

Rivelin

Named after a river that flows through the area. A 'rivulet' means small river.

Sandygate

Sandy road or path.

Shalesmoor

Said to be a boundary but I understand that it is to do with the geology of the area, built on shale.

Sharrow Vale

From word 'sherra', old English for shared land.

Sheffield 1737 by T. Oughtibridge

Sheffield

Clearing or treeless area by the river Sheaf. Sheffield was originally an Anglo Saxon settlement called Escafeld.

Shire Brook

Named after a river which is an old historical boundary separating the old kingdoms of Mercia and Northumbria. The river may have been known as 'Ochre Dyke'.

Shirecliffe

Bright steep hillside.

Shiregreen

Land or green on shire boundary.

Snig Hill

Snig Hill 1895 by A. Wilson

Takes its name from the practice of putting a 'snig' or length of wood through the back wheels of a cart going downhill in order to act as a brake.

Snig hill was, in the 17th century, a main route for heavily laden wagons. Nearby was a small workhouse and the children could earn a few pennies by helping the drivers slow down their wagons.

Sothall

Maybe Swota's area of land.

Southy Green

Simply South Green.

Stannington

Was known as 'Stanyton', thought to mean 'stone villa'. Roman remains have been found in the area so I'm not sure if it's relating to this period.

Stocksbridge

A Mr Stock may of owned the land where a wooden bridge crossed the Little Don.

Stradbroke

Named after a town in East Suffolk.

Tinsley

Tynni's mound.

Totley

Totley
Clearing of Tota's people.

Wadsley Bridge
Wade's forest clearing.

Wardsend
Corruption of 'Worldsend' because it is so isolated.

Walkley
From old English 'Walcas Leah' meaning Walca's forest clearing.

Waterthorpe
Viking farmstead by water.

Whirlow
With low meaning ancient monument it is possible that Whirlow means boundary mound.

Wisewood
Pasture or Meadow.

Wincobank
Wineca's woodland clearing.

Woodhouse
House in the wood.

Woodseats
Listed in the 13th century as Wodesets meaning houses in the woods. Worksop has a similar named area 'Woodsetts' which must have the same derivation.

Woodthorpe
Outlying farm near a wood. From Viking Norse.

Worrall

Believed to be from the Saxon word 'Hvirfull' meaning 'top' which when linked to the word 'Fjallsins' meant 'Top of the Hill'. In English with strong pronunciation of the letter 'R' it would soon have become 'Worrall'.

Wybourn

Maybe the mix of the Norse word 'Wy' for Willow and bourn meaning stream so 'stream with willow trees'. Legendary home of that fratenal greeting 'The Wybourn Kiss', i.e. a head butt!

Bibliography and Further Reading

	Author	ISBN
A Popular History of Sheffield	J Edward Vickers	0906787041
Street Names of Sheffield	Peter Harvey	1850480257
Sheffield's Time Trail: True Tales from the Norfolk Heritage Trail	Peter Machan	0901100528
The Making of Sheffield	Melvyn Jones	1903425425